Nonfiction

Nonfiction

Shane McCrae

Black
Lawrence
Press

Black
Lawrence
Press

www.blacklawrence.com

Executive Editor: Diane Goettel
Book and Cover Design: Amy Freels
Cover Art: "Untitled" by Jamie Newhall, © 2014

Copyright © 2014 Shane McCrae
ISBN: 978-1-937854-98-0

Black Lawrence Press
326 Bigham Street
Pittsburgh, PA 15211

Published 2014 by Black Lawrence Press.
Printed in the United States

Contents

What's merciful is not knowing where you are.
—Anthony Hecht

An Incident in the Life of Solomon Northup a Free Man

Spring it was spring was   spring in the morning spring

My wife whose skin is summer wheat

had gone

To cook at Sherrill's Coffee House whose   skin is wheat had gone

Over to Sandy Hill

My wife   Elizabeth my wife Anne   and Elizabeth

Our oldest daughter was

It spring in also spring in Sandy Hill

And Margaret and Alonzo with their aunt

At Saratoga I was walking in

The spring in the village of Saratoga Springs

And I I   loved my children no

Matter how dark their skin

I loved them as

if it were white

my wife whose skin is wheat

My wife whose skin is summer I

Was walking in the spring alone   two men approached

Two men approached and introduced themselves they

had been told

They said they had been told

I was an expert player on the violin

They said their names were Merrill Brown

And Abram Hamilton

They said they were associated with a circus had

Some trouble finding music for the circus

Asked   me to return with them to the circus

My wife would be   away for weeks

Whose skin is wheat and I had been

looking for work

And went with them

And I was drugged and sold in Washington DC

in the spring and only

Played only once

and made they   gave me more

Money than I had ever seen before

From any job before

and soon as I saw it   I should have known

It wasn't mine

They wouldn't let me keep it and it wasn't mine

Elizabeth whose skin is sun

Behind dark clouds it must be

I remember her skin wrong I

woke up in a box

With no

Windows and I was sitting on a bench   chained at my ankles and my wrists

To a large ring in the floor

it must be I remember wrong

Elizabeth wrong but

I could rebuild the chains now and the ring   the bench now and the room

From memory

The Visible Boy

1. How He Was Looked

And I had poked my penis through

a hole in the afghan I remember the

How he was looked   disgusted he

Looked angry and afraid

And I remember that was when it started   that he leaned

Over the back of the couch and put me in his mouth

And I was four or five it felt

Good and I wanted him

To yell at me or hit me and not do it anymore

And I had seen what he was doing

Before but it was women doing it

Before in magazines before

And I tried hard to copy it

The look of the men in the magazines   mouths

open eyes   closed or eyes open watching but I couldn't

watch   I / Tried

and I besides I thought   the men who weren't

watching looked happier

2. The Face of Someone

Seeing for someone

In the house   for company because

he what he does to my / Body he doesn't

want in the house

he hides the women in / He

hides the magazines in somewhere in   / Where guests would never go

for company he what he does to me

He wants to keep   private a me a secret   even then   / And even as a boy
    I knew

My body my / Black body wasn't

private wasn't   couldn't be

Secret and even then / I knew

He what he did to me   made me invisible   / I didn't have

the blond face of a kidnapped child I had

the face of someone

Who brought it on himself

3. Was Pretty Was Kids

Was pretty was kids

said I looked / Like Michael Jackson Michael Jackson 1982

And skinny sometimes   wouldn't eat for days

Was pretty and he saw it   was / Pretty he saw it too

Pretty for boys / To be a boy

Pretty it made him angry talked as if

It made him angry talked / Why

would I want to look like that / And didn't look at me   I thought

He didn't like me knew he

didn't like niggers and I was one   was half

Niggers and I was one   and wasn't also wasn't

old enough to be   afraid of him

the way a man   / Would

without love

he held me down face down

4. Playboy

Remember stripping in a quarry   or it was

A field of white

rocks piled in mounds / Four feet and five feet high

as tall as I was then

But no machinery

remember rode my bike / To the quarry to the field

And laid it down   on the rocks / In the middle of the summer on the
    warm rocks

thought / I would be beautiful

The way the women in the magazines / Were beautiful

naked on the rocks   and stripped   / And lay

down on the rocks   in the quarry in the field it was

In the middle of my neighborhood

I must have been   seven or eight

the rocks were sharp   / And swarming with fire ants

I lay there crying out

The Ambassador

Not African in Africa but here

In Africa belonging to

A tribe I anymore can't trace

But here the only growing up

Nigger on Broadmeade Avenue

in Round Rock Texas Africa

Or saw the others nowhere if

There anywhere were more

I go back and I see them

nowhere still

I go back in their skin

From the Greek

My son he was

Six he was six he's

ten now he was six

Six and he was

he had just gotten

In trouble six I don't

Remember what or

if he did

Anything or it was it me   he got

in trouble and he said   *I have the wrong*

Brain

and he didn't know

and doesn't still

what autism is

autism   from αὐτός   *self*

first used to mean

self-admiration

Essay on Sympathy on Envy

Melissa when   my wife when I

My wife went blind Melissa went

For a month was blind

and when after she   went blind it wasn't

Five days no more than three

And I already anybody I   / Saw I assumed was blind

I anybody in the street

saw and it took a moment had

To tell myself that person

probably wasn't   / Blind and it was it

every time a shock

To realize that person   probably wasn't and it was

always a shock   / Remembering Melissa was

Not that I ever tried to stop

Ever no anybody not

even a single child

From stepping into traffic

An Incident in the Life of David Blount a Slave

The days on the plantation was the happy days

We didn't mind the work so much   because the ground was soft as ashes

hot / Days we would all stop work about

Three in the evening   and go swimming in the river

one time there / I

done forgot the year

some white men came   / Down the river in a boat / They come

Into the fields and talks to us

They says our master isn't treating us

right and they says / We ought to be

paid for our work

I laughs at them but some

Fool niggers listen

it appears these men / Give them some guns

after I left and them / Fool niggers listen   hold

a meeting the next day   in the pack house

So I is lying

Up in the loft and I

Hear them say   they going up to the big house

And kill the whole family

I go

Out the window tell the master me / And him

run out to the pack house   and quick as lightning

I slam the door shut / The master

locks them niggers in

And then the master   yells he yells *I'se got*

Men and guns out here

throw your guns out

the hole up there in the loft   I know

How many guns they got

I count 'em as they throw 'em out

Well   the master keeps them shut

up for about a week   / On short rations

and at / The end of that

Time he says   *Dave* he says to me   *I reckon them*

niggers am cured for good

And burns the pack house down

How to Survive Desire

1. You Will Want a Longer Mattress

When placed   when you are placed   confined when you

When you are put in the hole

When you are put in Ad. Seg. in

Administrative Segregation you

Will need to use your blankets as   / Your blankets

so as not to freeze

And you will need to wear your clothes

When sleeping so as not to freeze

You won't be able to

fashion a pillow from your blankets or your clothes and pil-

lows are so rare

Although you will be / Issued a pillowcase you will be

Consider rolling one end of your mattress for

Use as a pillow you might find

you need to curl up like a fe-

tus

which is a warmer way to sleep

2. You Will Want to Seal the Door of Your Cell

A breeze will sometimes gets

from nowhere in   / And some

particles sometimes dust and even in-

sects and you will

Sometimes a fellow prisoner will kick a shank

Under your door

and you will want   to hide from also what-

ever he's hiding from   / But not with him

And sometimes dust

insects and even rodents rats   / And did you know

rats are the dust of animals   / Like how

dust is the dust of dirt

Insects and e-

ven rodents   rats / Sometimes and you will want

to slow the water down

when the floods come which come remember

prisoner your Ark

Is already at the bottom of the sea

3. You Will Want to Make a Muff Bag

It's what you sounds like think it is

Achieved by filling plastic bags   / Two

garbage bags

Tying the bags together

Filling the bags with water / The bags   or call it now the bags the body

For each of the bags use   two bags as

It has a tendency to puncture

at your wildest and most concentrated moment warm / Water

you filled the bags with warm

Water warm water soaks your bunk

And suddenly your body is ridiculous

your bed is cold

Don't be embarrassed

prisoner we've all   / Been there before   scrambling for fresh

sheets dry sheets / It   takes a few bodies to know how much water is too much water how much force

Is too much force

Prisoner   your own body

is the only body

you can't change

Essay on I Pause in the Middle of Writing a Poem to Write This Essay

Nothing to say was anyway was wrong

wrong about language anyway was wrong

Wrong about anyway it was   anyway and you've had it

wrong for anyway

You've had it anyway and anyway / Making   you anyway when

you are you're the furthest from

Being made anything a little even by anything

But making you affirm   you make   the evidence

up to that moment you've been made

By anything and afterward

you most do not exist

Even in the middle of

making to come

especially then

4. You Will Want to Cover the Vent or Vents in Your Cell

Nothing in breathe in nothing in

The *start* in *startle*   the French ending

prisoner your breath is / Half of your face

At least half and the guards control

The flow of air   into your cell / The temperature of coming in

The *come* you see it almost in *control*

The warden and the guards the *come* in there hidden in there

Like how your body is   hidden in the air   and you can't see the air

the warden and the guards   / You see their faces

And waste your anger there   your feeling of

powerlessness

Prisoner they control you with   something invisible

Understand you are powerless to fight it

Fight it

An Incident in the Life of Solomon Northup a Free Man

Woke for the first   time in my life

chained aching woke in darkness

Woke in a dark my eyes

Couldn't adjust to woke

chained to a ring in the floor

Head aching   chained in a dark room

And hearing footsteps voices

overhead I realized

The room was underground

Woke   and at first I couldn't

Remember how I came   to be in the room   and after I

After remembering the men   who ran the circus the

Two white men who   with whom

I had been traveling

Remembered but I couldn't understand

remembered only

Eagerness   kindness in their faces

As they handed me the money I had earned

And kindness in their faces as they left me for the night

And woke in darkness was

In darkness for   hours and no one came

I felt my way

around the room I found

The ring in the floor remembered

but I couldn't understand I   felt my way around

Crawling   and in the darkness

I after a while   couldn't be sure

My eyes were open

Notes

The two poems titled "An Incident in the Life of Solomon Northup a Free Man" rely upon Solomon Northup's *Twelve Years a Slave* for many of their details.

"An Incident in the Life of David Blount a Slave" was adapted from David Blount's untitled slave narrative.

"How to Survive Desire" is based on *Prisoners' Inventions*, by Angelo; "You Will Want a Longer Mattress" is adapted from the first essay in that book, "Pillows." "How to Survive Desire" is dedicated to Matthew Salesses.

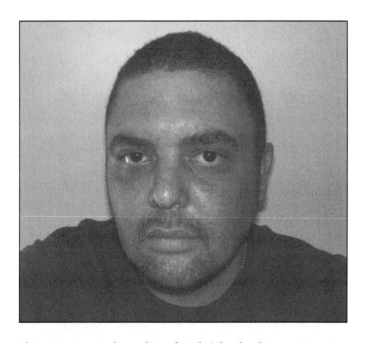

Shane McCrae is the author of *Mule* (Cleveland State University Poetry Center, 2011), a finalist for the Kate Tufts Discovery Award and the PEN Center USA Literary Award, *Blood* (Noemi Press, 2013), and *Forgiveness Forgiveness* (Factory Hollow Press, 2014), as well as two chapbooks, *One Neither One* (Octopus Books, 2009) and *In Canaan* (Rescue Press, 2010). His work has appeared in *The Best American Poetry, The American Poetry Review, Fence, Gulf Coast, jubilat* and others, and he has received a Whiting Writer's Award and a fellowship from the NEA. He teaches in the brief-residency MFA program at Spalding University.

Acknowledgments

Thanks to everyone at Black Lawrence Press, especially Kit Frick and Diane Goettel, for all their help. Thanks also to Derek Gromadzki and Melissa McCrae for the same. And thanks to the editors and staffs of the following journals, in which some of these poems first appeared, sometimes in different versions:

The American Poetry Review: "Essay on I Pause in the Middle of Writing a Poem to Write This Essay"

Bellingham Review: "An Incident in the Life of Solomon Northup a Free Man" ("Spring it was spring was")

Boston Review: "The Face of Someone"

jubilat: "Was Pretty Was Kids"

Likestarlings: "You Will Want to Seal the Door of Your Cell" and "You Will Want to Cover the Vent or Vents in Your Cell"

Paperbag: "Playboy"

RealPoetik: "An Incident in the Life of Solomon Northup a Free Man" ("Woke for the first")

Tuba: "Essay on Sympathy on Envy" and "From the Greek"

Verse Wisconsin: "An Incident in the Life of David Blount a Slave"

Washington Square: "You Will Want to Make a Muff Bag"

My gratitude to the Mrs. Giles Whiting Foundation and the National Endowment for the Arts for their support.